How to
Count
Sheep
Without
Falling Asleep

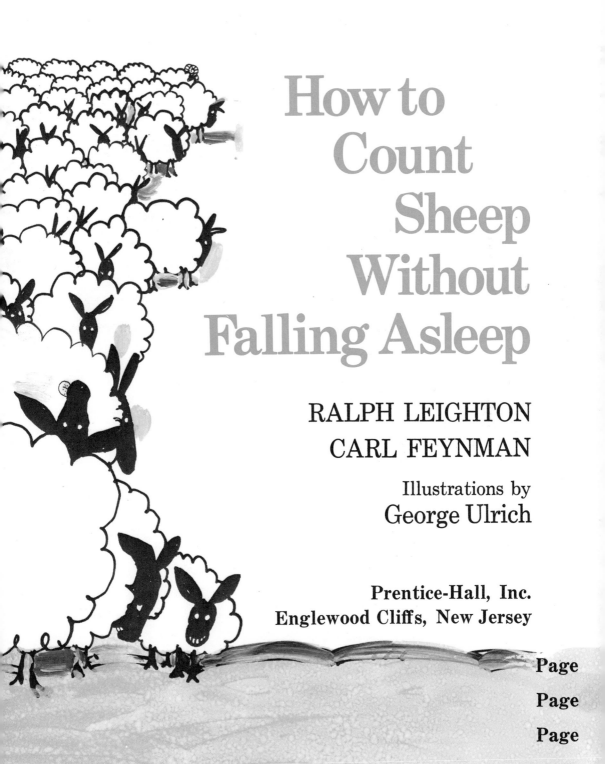

How to Count Sheep Without Falling Asleep

RALPH LEIGHTON
CARL FEYNMAN

Illustrations by
George Ulrich

Prentice-Hall, Inc.
Englewood Cliffs, New Jersey

Page

Page

Page

Prentice-Hall International, Inc., London
Prentice-Hall of Australia, Pty. Ltd., North Sydney
Prentice-Hall of Canada, Ltd., Toronto
Prentice-Hall of India Private Ltd., New Delhi
Prentice-Hall of Japan, Inc., Tokyo

10 9 8 7 6 5 4 3 2 1

Library of Congress Cataloging in Publication Data

Leighton, Ralph.
  How to count sheep without falling asleep.

    SUMMARY: Explores the concept of using symbols
for numbers: ones, tens, hundreds, etc.
    1. Numeration — Juvenile literature. (1. Number
systems) I. Feynman, Carl, joint author. (1. Number
systems) I. Feynman, Carl, joint author. II. Ulrich,
George. III. Title.
QA141.3.L43   513'.2   76-10237
ISBN: 0-13-404459-2

Long, long ago, people didn't need numbers: life was simpler then. Cavepeople killed a snake or a mammoth or a sabre-toothed tiger in order to eat. They knew when there was *enough* food and when there was *not enough* food; they didn't need to know exactly how many dead snakes they had in the cave.

Later, cavepeople developed different clubs for killing different animals more easily. That's called progress.

These new weapons made people better hunters. Now they could kill mammoth mammoth,

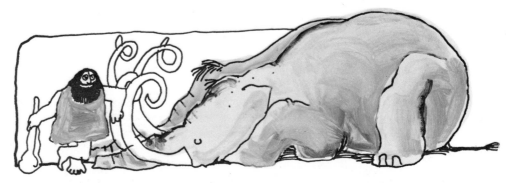

or sabre-toothed tiger sabre-toothed tiger sabre-toothed tiger,

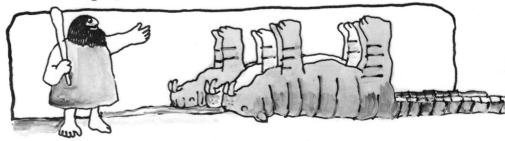

or snake snake snake snake snake snake snake.

Page

Page

Page

Page

Page

Page

Much later, people learned to keep animals
in flocks, so they didn't have to chase them in order
to kill them for food. Then they needed to know
exactly how many they had.
At first the shepherd counted his sheep by notching
his stick, but when a sheep died, he couldn't
un-notch it.

Then he tried counting his sheep by putting small rocks in a sack, one rock for each sheep.
But when his herd got bigger, he couldn't carry the sack anymore.

So he used a black rock ● to replace ⊙⊙⊙⊙ ⊙⊙⊙⊙⊙⊙. So ●●◆ ⊙⊙⊙ was the same as ⊙⊙⊙⊙⊙⊙⊙⊙⊙⊙⊙⊙⊙⊙⊙⊙⊙⊙⊙⊙ , except that it weighed less.

This was a good idea, but he still needed to empty the sack and count all the rocks every time he wanted to know how many sheep he had, and he could never be certain that some of the rocks hadn't fallen out of the sack.

His next idea was to chip the number of sheep into a stone, using **|** for each white rock and **X** for each black one: **XXXX |||**.

Now he had the same problem he had with the notched stick: what to do when a sheep dies? So he invented a mark to mean take away. When a sheep died, he chipped – I ; if three sheep were sold, he chipped – III .

But what if ||| sheep strayed from the flock? He figured out that he would have to change an X to ||||| ||||| and then take away ||| .

And then if ||| sheep wandered back with a new lamb, he would change ||||| ||||| into X | .

Now the shepherd could add or subtract numbers as long as he remembered to change X into ||||| ||||| and ||||| ||||| into X when necessary.

XIII

One day the Emperor came and ordered the shepherd to count all the sheep in the village so he could tax the shepherds according to the size of their flocks.

The stone the shepherd made for the Emperor
looked like this:

The shepherd remembered that when he had too many white rocks in his sack, he used a black rock to represent ○○○○○○○○○○ , and when he had ‖‖‖ ‖/‖ , he used ✕ instead. Now he invented the symbol Ϲ instead of ✕✕✕✕✕ ✕✕✕✕✕.

So he changed ✕✕✕✕✕ ✕✕✕✕✕ to ϹϹϹ.
✕✕✕✕✕ ✕✕✕✕✕
✕ ✕ ✕✕✕ ✕✕✕✕✕

Now the shepherd could add bigger numbers than ever before. His system worked so well that all the other shepherds asked him to keep track of their flocks for them.

He used the numbers so much that soon he knew all the combinations: he knew that I and I is always II, and II and II is IIII. He also knew that IIII minus II is II, and II minus I is I. It became so easy for him that he wanted to show all the other shepherds, so they could keep track of their own flocks.

II and II is IIII.

Since they didn't know how to add and subtract, the shepherd invented a machine to help them. To add IIII and IIIII, he put the arrow under the first number, found the second number on the *sliding part*, and read the answer directly *below* the second number.

To subtract ⅼⅼⅼⅼⅼ from ⅼⅼ⫻ⅼⅼ ⫻ⅼⅼⅼ, the shepherd worked backwards, from the bottom up, so the answer was directly *above* the arrow.

The shepherd was very proud of his new invention.
But it couldn't give an answer larger than **X**, so
he made another slide rule using **X** instead of **I**.

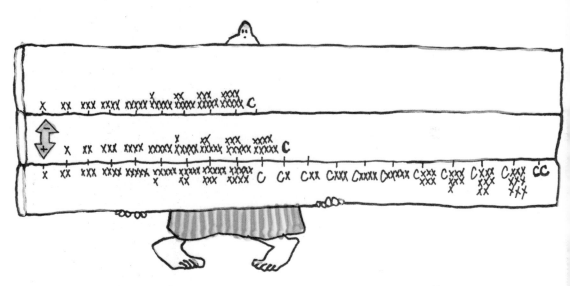

He made *another* slide rule using **C** instead of **I**,
and he invented a new symbol **M** for **CCCCC**
CCCCC.

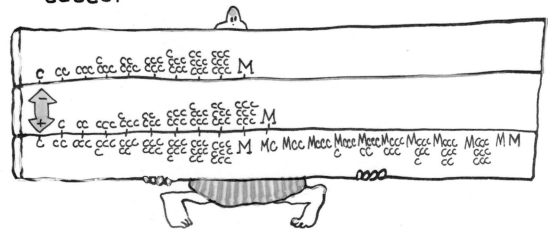

Then the shepherd tried a big addition problem
with all three machines:

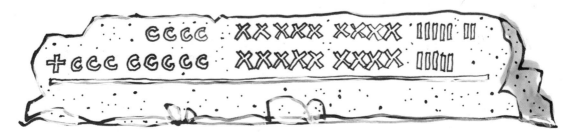

First he added the **I** on the **I** slide rule.

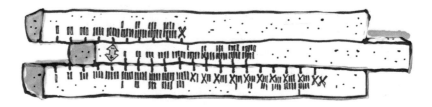

Then he added the **X** on the **X** slide rule.

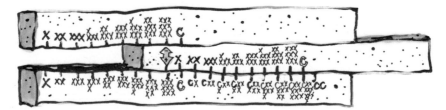

Then he added the C on the C slide rule.
His answer was **M CCC XXXXXX II**

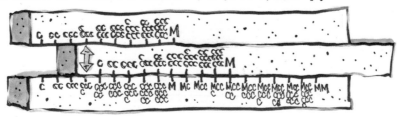

"There must be a better system," thought the shepherd to himself. "I still have to count a lot of 1's and X's and C's and M's. I need to develop a different symbol for each number, so I can tell | | | | | | | | from | | | | | | | | at a glance, without counting all those | s."

He started chipping out new numbers. One **I** was a line with one angle, two **II**s was a line with two angles, three **III**s was a line with three angles and so on. It worked pretty well. Now the shepherd Now the shepherd could tell at a glance the difference between **IIIIII** and **IIIIIII**: **6** and **7**.

Then he noticed that he only needed nine I s because ten I s were X. He only needed nine X s because ten X s were C. He only needed nine C s because ten C s were M.

"Why not write how many I s, X s, C s and M s there are using the new numbers? Then I'll only need to memorize I I I I I I I I I new symbols!"

So he chipped out a sample to see how the numbers worked.

The Emperor heard about the new system and ordered the shepherd to show the tax collectors how to use them.

But when tax time came, it was clear that there was a flaw in the new system. The tax collectors couldn't tell the difference between 12 (**XII**) and 12 (**CII**) and 12 (**CXX**) and 12 (**MCC**) sheep. Of course, it made a big difference to the shepherds!

The Emperor was very angry so the shepherd had to think fast. With his new symbols the shepherd could show how *many* |s, Xs, Cs and Ms appeared in each number. Now he needed something to show that there were none of the symbols in a number. So he invented an empty looking mark O to show that a column was empty. He showed the Emperor how the O solved the problem.

Then he chipped out another stone, leaving out all the s at the beginning of numbers.

Then he tried some addition and subtraction with the ◯'s. The problems were very easy:

This latest invention pleased the Emperor, so the shepherd was free to go home and make yet another slide rule, using his new numbers.

As soon as he finished making the new machine,
he tried a big addition problem:

First, he added the I's:

Next, he added the X's:

Then, he added the C's:

Next he tried a big subtraction problem on the slide rule.

The shepherd didn't know how to subtract 5 from 2, so he borrowed ||\|| ||\|| from the ✕ column, and then subtracted 5 from 12.

Next, he subtracted the X's. Since an
X was borrowed to make ||||||||||| ,
there were only 5 X's left.
Then, he subtracted the C's.

The shepherd added and subtracted so many numbers that after a while he didn't need to use his machine anymore: he knew all the combinations by heart.

To make your own slide rule adding and subtracting machine, follow these directions carefully. You will find that after a while *you* won't need it anymore either.

DIRECTIONS FOR ADDING AND SUBTRACTING MACHINE

You will need a piece of blank cardboard, a pencil, a ruler with centimeter markings, and a pair of scissors.

Mark both edges of the paper at 2, 4, 6 and 8 centimeters from the top.

Draw parallel lines connecting the marks.

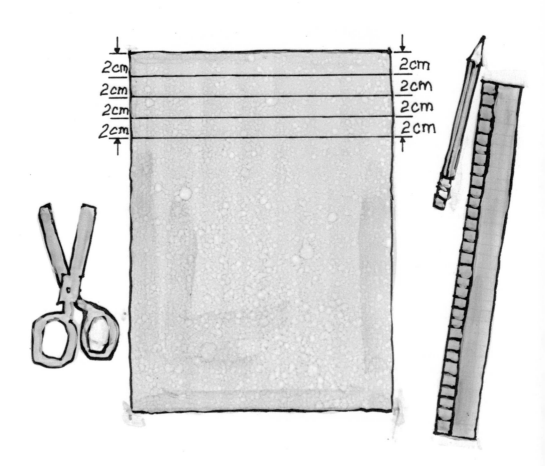

Mark by centimeters and number carefully
as follows:
From 1 to 10 *above* the first line; from 1 to 20 *below*
the second line; from 1 to 10 *above* the last line,
giving the first mark to the arrow.

Cut carefully along the last two lines, and place the
sliding part between the first and second lines.

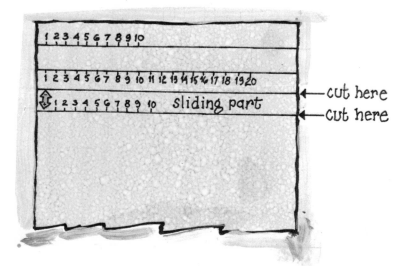

—cut here

—cut here

Your finished machine should look like this:

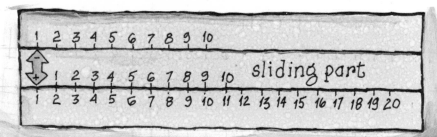

You are now ready to do your own adding and
subtracting. *Have fun!*